I0455418

May 2013

CORPORATE INCOME TAX

Effective Tax Rates Can Differ Significantly from the Statutory Rate

May 2013

CORPORATE INCOME TAX

Effective Tax Rates Can Differ Significantly from the Statutory Rate

Why GAO Did This Study

Proponents of lowering the U.S. corporate income tax rate commonly point to evidence that the U.S. statutory corporate tax rate of 35 percent, as well as its average effective tax rate, which equals the amount of income tax corporations pay divided by their pretax income, are high relative to other countries. However, GAO's 2008 report on corporate tax liabilities (GAO-08-957) found that nearly 55 percent of all large U.S.-controlled corporations reported no federal tax liability in at least one year between 1998 and 2005.

Given the difficult budget choices Congress faces and its need to know corporations' share of the overall tax burden, GAO was asked to assess the extent to which corporations are paying U.S. corporate income tax. In this report, among other things, GAO (1) defines average corporate ETR and describes the common methods and data used to estimate this rate and (2) estimates average ETRs based on financial statement reporting and tax reporting. To conduct this work, GAO reviewed economic and accounting literature, analyzed income and expense data that large corporations report on the Schedules M-3 that they file with Internal Revenue Service (IRS), and interviewed IRS officials.

What GAO Recommends

GAO does not make recommendations in this report. GAO provided a draft of this report to IRS for review and comment. IRS provided technical comments which were incorporated as appropriate.

View GAO-13-520. For more information, contact James R. White at (202) 512-9110 or whitej@gao.gov.

What GAO Found

Effective tax rates (ETR) differ from statutory tax rates in that they attempt to measure taxes paid as a proportion of economic income, while statutory rates indicate the amount of tax liability (before any credits) relative to taxable income, which is defined by tax law and reflects tax benefits and subsidies built into the law. Lacking access to detailed data from tax returns, most researchers have estimated ETRs based on data from financial statements. A common measure of tax liability used in past estimates has been the current tax expense—either federal only or worldwide (which comprises federal, foreign, and U.S. state and local income taxes). The most common measure of income for these estimates has been some variant of pretax net book income. GAO was able to compare book tax expenses to tax liabilities actually reported on corporate income tax returns.

For tax year 2010 (the most recent information available), profitable U.S. corporations that filed a Schedule M-3 paid U.S. federal income taxes amounting to about 13 percent of the pretax worldwide income that they reported in their financial statements (for those entities included in their tax returns). When foreign and state and local income taxes are included, the ETR for profitable filers increases to around 17 percent. The inclusion of unprofitable firms, which pay little if any tax, also raises the ETRs because the losses of unprofitable corporations greatly reduce the denominator of the measures. Even with the inclusion of unprofitable filers, which increased the average worldwide ETR to 22.7 percent, all of the ETRs were well below the top statutory tax rate of 35 percent. GAO could only estimate average ETRs with the data available and could not determine the variation in rates across corporations. The limited available data from Schedules M-3, along with prior GAO work relating to corporate taxpayers, suggest that ETRs are likely to vary considerably across corporations.

Comparison of Alternative Measures of Average Effective Tax Rates for Schedule M-3 Filers, Tax Year 2010

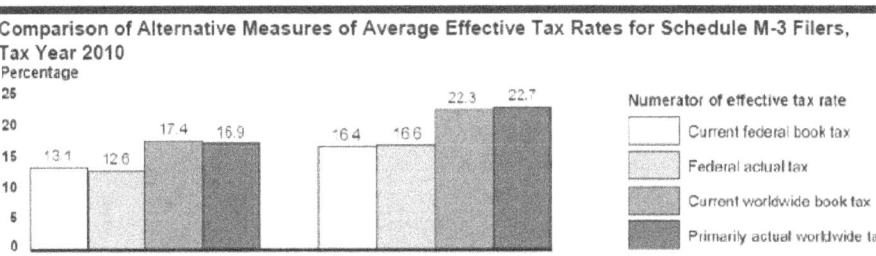

Source: GAO analysis of IRS data.

Contents

Figures

GAO U.S. GOVERNMENT ACCOUNTABILITY OFFICE

441 G St. N.W.
Washington, DC 20548

May 30, 2013

The Honorable Carl Levin
Chairman
Permanent Subcommittee on Investigations
Committee on Homeland Security
    and Governmental Affairs
United States Senate

The Honorable Tom Coburn, M.D.
Ranking Member
Committee on Homeland Security
    and Governmental Affairs
United States Senate

Proponents of lowering the U.S. corporate income tax rate commonly point to evidence that the U.S. statutory federal corporate income tax rate of 35 percent, as well as its average effective tax rate (ETR), which equals the amount of income tax corporations pay divided by their pretax income, are high relative to other countries. However, our 2008 report on corporate income tax liabilities found that nearly 55 percent of all large U.S.-controlled corporations reported no federal tax liability in at least one year between 1998 and 2005.[1]

Statutory tax rates provide only a limited measure of the share of income that businesses pay in taxes because many other aspects of the tax system, such as exemptions, deferrals, tax credits, and other forms of incentives, also determine the amount of tax that a business ultimately pays on its income. The average effective tax rate reflects the combined effects of all these tax system components. However, obtaining the data to calculate ETRs is challenging. The two typical sources, tax returns and financial statements, both have limitations.

Given the difficult budget choices Congress faces and its need to know corporations' share of the overall tax burden, you asked us to assess the extent to which corporations are paying U.S. corporate income tax. In this

---

[1]GAO, *Tax Administration: Comparison of the Reported Tax Liabilities of Foreign- and U.S.-Controlled Corporations, 1998-2005* (Washington, D.C.: July 24, 2008).

GAO-13-520 Corporate Income Tax

report, we (1) explain the definition of average corporate ETR and the common methods and data used to estimate this rate, (2) estimate average ETRs based on financial statement reporting and tax reporting, and (3) describe the largest sources of the differences in income reported on financial statements and tax returns.

To explain how the average corporate effective tax rate is defined and to describe the common methods and data used to estimate this rate, we reviewed and summarized the relevant economic literature. (See app. I for a summary of past studies that used financial statement data to estimate average effective tax rates.)

To report what available data indicate about the difference between average effective tax rates based on financial statement reporting versus those based on tax reporting, we computed a variety of such rates using income and expense data that large corporations report on the Schedules M-3 that they file with the Internal Revenue Service (IRS). (These schedules reconcile income and expense amounts the corporations report for financial statement purposes to amounts they report for tax purposes.) These data, which the joint Treasury-IRS M-3 First Look Team compiles for a large sample of taxpayers, enabled us to estimate and compare U.S. and worldwide effective tax rates on worldwide income using only financial statement data; U.S. effective tax rates on worldwide income using only data reported for tax purposes; and U.S. and worldwide effective tax rates on worldwide income using income data from financial statements and tax return data for the amount of taxes paid.[2] Our estimates of effective tax rates are limited to corporations with assets of $10 million or more (which are the ones that file Schedule M-3) and primarily to tax years 2008 through 2010 because those are the only

---

[2]The measure of worldwide income from the Schedule M-3 represents the worldwide financial statement income of the U.S. corporation filing the M-3 and any entities included in its tax return.

years for which IRS has compiled data separately for corporations that had nonnegative values for net income on their financial statements.[3]

To identify common differences between financial statement reporting and tax reporting, we reviewed the relevant economic and accounting literature and obtained data from IRS on the dollar magnitude of those differences that are reported in detail on Schedule M-3. The data we report on differences between financial statement and tax return items cover tax years 2006 through 2010. While there are limitations to the data provided on the Schedule M-3 and general reporting problems with tax return data, we determined that the data were reliable for our purposes after reviewing relevant documentation and discussing quality control procedures with IRS officials.

We conducted our work from March 2012 to May 2013 in accordance with all sections of GAO's Quality Assurance Framework that are relevant to our objectives. The framework requires that we plan and perform the engagement to obtain sufficient and appropriate evidence to meet our stated objectives and to discuss any limitations in our work. We believe that the information and data obtained, and the analysis conducted, provide a reasonable basis for any findings and conclusions in this product.

---

[3]The Schedule M-3 data are drawn from IRS's Statistics of Income division's annual stratified random samples of corporate tax returns. The results we present based on these samples are subject to sampling error. We do not have the detailed information needed to estimate the size of the sampling error; however, we believe these errors are negligible because a significant proportion of the Schedule M-3 filers is sampled at a 100 percent rate and the remaining M-3 filers are sampled at rates of 27 percent or more. Those sampled at the 100 percent rate accounted for 99 percent of the total assets of this population for 2010. The data sets for the Schedule M-3 differ from the Statistics of Income corporate sample data sets in that only returns reporting assets of $10 million or more are considered in the Schedule M-3 data sets, and returns that do not meet simple reconciliation rules between M-3 Parts I and II and between M-3 Parts III and II are dropped from those data sets. Our analysis excludes pass-through entities, which do not pay income tax. Their income is passed through to their shareholders or partners where it is taxed under applicable income tax. [Pass through entities include partnerships, which do not have shareholders. Also, corporations or other entities can be partners or shareholders in pass through entities.]

Background

Corporate Income Tax

The base of the federal corporate income tax includes net income from business operations (receipts, minus the costs of purchased goods, labor, interest, and other expenses). It also includes net income that corporations earn in the form of interest, dividends, rent, royalties, and realized capital gains. The statutory rate of tax on net corporate income ranges from 15 to 35 percent, depending on the amount of income earned.[4] The United States taxes the worldwide income of domestic corporations, regardless of where the income is earned, with a foreign tax credit for certain taxes paid to other countries. The timing of the tax liability depends on several factors. For example, income earned not by the domestic corporation, but by a foreign subsidiary is generally not taxed until a distribution—such as a dividend—is made to the U.S. corporation.[5]

At about $242 billion, corporate income taxes are far smaller than the $845 billion in social insurance taxes and $1.1 trillion in individual income taxes that the Office of Management and Budget (OMB) estimates were paid in fiscal year 2012 to fund the federal government.[6] Figure 1 shows the relative distribution of federal taxes.

---

[4]26 U.S.C. § 11. In addition, present law imposes an alternative minimum tax (AMT) on certain corporations to the extent that their minimum tax liability exceeds their regular tax liability. 26 U.S.C. § 56. In general, the AMT applies a lower tax rate to a broader tax base. Specifically, the regular tax base is increased for AMT purposes by adding back certain items treated as tax preferences and disallowing certain deductions and credits. Also, marginal rates are higher over limited income ranges to recapture the benefits of the rates below 35 percent.

[5] Taxable income is total income, including taxable income from foreign sources, minus deductions such as for salaries and wages, depreciation, and net operating loss carryovers. The next step is to calculate the tentative tax owed (taxable income times the applicable rate). The last step is to subtract any tax credits, including the foreign tax credit, to get the taxes owed.

[6]Office of Management and Budget, *Historical Tables, Budget of the United States Government, Fiscal Year 2014* (Washington, D.C.: Apr. 2013).

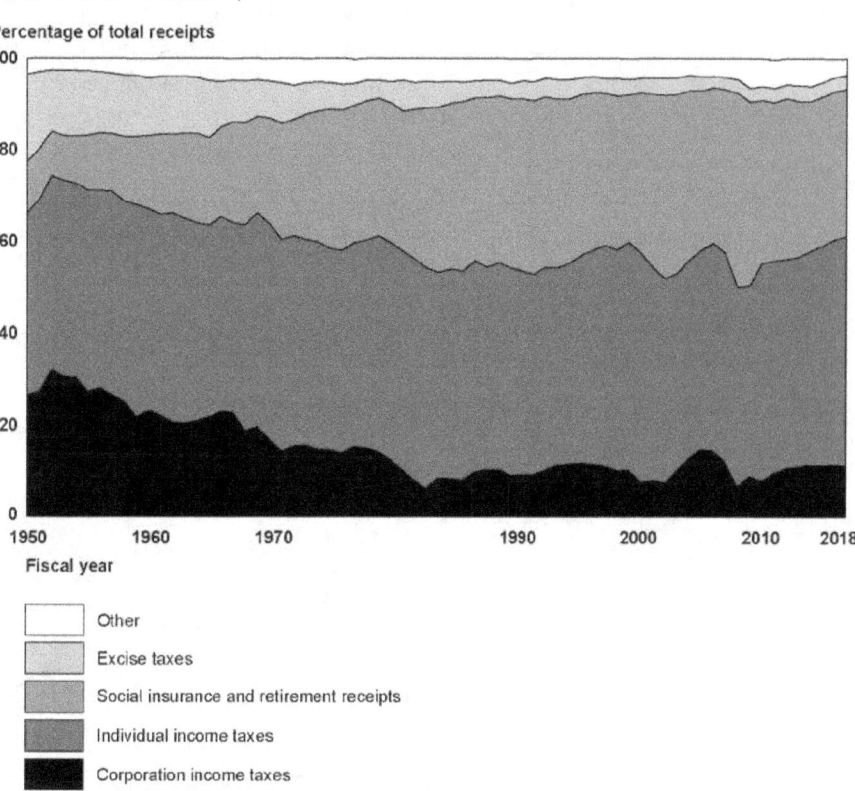

Figure 1: Federal Tax Revenues as a Percentage of Total Receipts, 1950 to 2012 (2013 to 2018 Estimated)

Percentage of total receipts

Fiscal year

- Other
- Excise taxes
- Social insurance and retirement receipts
- Individual income taxes
- Corporation income taxes

Source: GAO representation of OMB data

Figures 1 and 2 show the trend in corporate income tax revenues since 1950. According to tax experts, corporate income tax revenues fell from the 1960s to the early 1980s for several reasons. For example, corporate income became a smaller share of gross domestic product (GDP) during these years, partly due to the fact that corporate debt, and therefore deductible interest payments, increased relative to corporate equity, reducing the tax base. In addition, tax expenditures, such as more generous depreciation rules also grew over that period.[7] Since the early 1980s, the corporate income tax has accounted for about 6 to 15 percent

---

[7]C. Eugene Steuerle, *Contemporary U.S. Tax Policy* (Washington, D.C.: The Urban Institute Press, 2004); and Jane G. Gravelle, "The Corporate Tax: Where Has It Been and Where Is It Going?" *National Tax Journal*, vol. 57, no. 4 (2004): 903-23.

of federal revenue. Consequently, although not the largest, it remains an important source of federal revenue. Relative to GDP, the corporate income tax has ranged from a little over 1 percent to just under 2.7 percent during those same years, as shown in figure 2. The Congressional Budget Office (CBO) recently projected that despite the recent uptick, corporate income tax revenue for the next 10 years as a percentage of GDP is expected to stay within this same range.[8]

Figure 2: Federal Tax Revenues as a Percentage of GDP, 1950 to 2012 (2013 to 2018 Estimated)

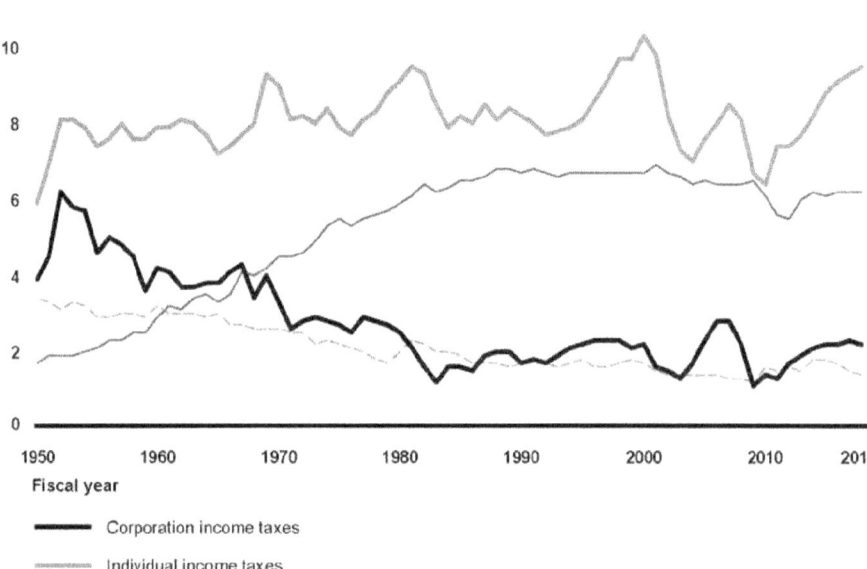

Source: GAO representation of OMB data

---

[8]Congressional Budget Office, *The Budget and Economic Outlook: Fiscal Years 2013-2023* (Washington, D.C.: February 2013).

GAO-13-520 Corporate Income Tax

Financial and Tax Reporting Requirements for Corporations

Businesses operating as publicly traded corporations in the United States are required to report the income they earn and the expenses (including taxes) they incur each year according to two separate standards. First, they must produce financial statements in accordance with generally accepted accounting principles (GAAP), based on standards established by the Financial Accounting Standards Board. Income and expense items reported in these statements are commonly known as book items. Second, in general, domestic corporations, including publicly traded corporations, must file corporate income tax returns on which they report income, expenses, and tax liabilities according to rules set out in the Internal Revenue Code (IRC) and associated Department of Treasury regulations.[9]

The IRC generally requires that a corporation's taxable year and overall method of accounting conform to those used for financial reporting purposes. However, many specific differences are permitted (and, in some cases, required) between financial accounting and tax accounting. The differences are referred to as book-tax differences. The primary purpose of financial reporting is to provide GAAP information to investors and creditors, recognizing that some of that information must be based on judgment and estimates.[10] In contrast, the primary purpose of tax accounting is to measure income for the purpose of imposing the federal income tax. Tax reporting rules incline towards objectivity, administrability, and consistency among taxpayers. The tax code is also used as a fiscal and social policy tool, incorporating incentives to encourage certain taxpayer behaviors, such as investment and research. Such incentives generally cause deviations between book income and taxable income. In addition, the federal income tax expenses that corporations report in their financial statements for a given year do not necessarily reflect the actual tax liabilities and payments that they

---

[9]Except as otherwise noted, references to tax accounting refer to this second set of rules. Also, unless otherwise noted, we use the term taxes actually paid in reference to the income tax liabilities (after credits) that corporations report on their federal income tax return each year.

[10] The measurement of business net income is inherently difficult and some components of both tax and book net income are estimates subject to some imprecision. (Net income equals total income minus expenses.) One important source of imprecision is the difficulty of measuring costs associated with the use of capital assets. Both book and tax depreciation rules allocate capital costs over the expected useful lives of different types of assets. The actual useful life of specific assets may differ from the expected lives used for purposes of either book or tax depreciation.

GAO-13-520 Corporate Income Tax

reported on their federal tax return for that year. In financial statements, income tax expense includes the estimated future tax effects attributable to temporary differences between book and tax income.

Prior to 2004, corporations were required to reconcile their book net income with tax net income reporting on Schedule M-1 of their income tax returns by comparing the book and tax return amounts of a limited number of income and expense items. Concern over the growing difference observed between pretax book net income and tax net income and the lack of detail available from the Schedule M-1 on the sources of these differences led to the development of the more extensive reporting on book-tax differences that is now required on Schedule M-3.[11] One important concern with Schedule M-1 arose from the fact that GAAP governing which components of large multinational corporate groups need to be included in financial statements differ from tax rules that specify which of those components need to be included in consolidated tax returns. Consequently, the financial statement data that taxpayers reported on their M-1s could relate to a much different business entity from the one covered by the tax return. A Schedule M-3 filer is now required to report the worldwide income of the entity represented in its financial statements and then follow a well-defined series of steps—subtracting out income and losses of foreign and U.S. entities that are included in the financial statements but not in consolidated tax returns; adding in the income and losses of entities that are included in consolidated tax returns but not in financial statements; and making other adjustments to arrive at the book income of tax-includible entities. The Schedule M-3 also requires filers to report many more specific income and expense items according to both financial statement and tax rules than the M-1 required. The items causing the largest book-tax differences are identified later in this report. (See app. II for a copy of the Schedule M-3.)

---

[11]These requirements, which apply to all corporations with assets that equal or exceed $10 million, became effective December 2004.

Past Studies Estimating Corporate Effective Tax Rates Used a Range of Data Sources and Methodologies for a Variety of Reasons

Alternative Corporate Effective Tax Rates Are Designed to Address Different Questions

Effective tax rates on corporate income can be defined in a variety of ways, each of which provides insights into a different issue. These rates fall into two broad categories—average rates and marginal rates. An average corporate effective tax rate, which is the focus of this report, is generally computed as the ratio of taxes paid or tax liabilities accrued in a given year over the net income the corporation earned that year; it is a good summary of the corporation's overall tax burden on income earned during that particular period. "Burden" in this context refers to what the corporation remits to the Treasury, also called statutory burden. However, statutory burden may differ from economic burden, which measures the loss of after-tax income due to a tax. The economic burden of some or all of the taxes on a corporation may be shifted to the firm's customers or workers, as well as to other firms and other workers. Any remaining burden is borne by the corporation's shareholders or other owners of capital. A marginal effective tax rate focuses on the tax burden associated with a specific investment (usually over the full life of that investment) and is a better measure of the effects that taxes have on incentives to invest.[12] Effective rates differ from statutory tax rates in that they attempt to measure taxes paid as a proportion of economic income, while

---

[12]In contrast, the income included in an average effective tax rate computation may be derived from investments made in many different past years in addition to all those made in the current year; it does not include estimates of any income to be earned in the future. Some researchers have also developed a measure they call the effective average tax rate, which is a weighted average of the statutory tax rate and the effective marginal tax rate to study the effects of taxes on decisions relating to large, discrete investments in contrast to those about small differences in the size of a particular investment. (See, for example, Michael Devereux and Rachel Griffith, "Taxes and the Location of Production: Evidence from a Panel of US Multinationals," *Journal of Public Economics,* vol. 68 (June 1998): 335-367.)

statutory rates indicate the amount of tax liability (before any credits) relative to taxable income, which is defined by tax law and reflects tax benefits and subsidies built into the law. The statutory tax rate of 35 percent applying to most large U.S. corporations is sometimes referred to as the "headline rate," because it is the rate most familiar to the public.

Data from Schedule M-3 of the Federal Corporate Income Tax Return Allow for More Accurate Comparisons of Effective Tax Rates Based on Alternative Reporting Rules

Until recently, data constraints have inhibited comparisons of effective tax rate estimates based on the alternative reporting systems. Access to tax return data is tightly restricted by law; consequently, most researchers who have estimated average effective tax rates for U.S. corporations have used either firm-level or aggregated data compiled from corporate financial statements for their measures of both tax liability and income. Even those with access to tax data could not easily determine how effective tax rates based on financial statements would differ from those based on actual tax returns because, as noted above, the scope of the business entity represented in a corporation's financial statement can be quite different from that covered by its consolidated federal tax return.[13] Researchers with access to data from Schedule M-3 and other parts of corporate income tax returns will now be able to directly compare effective tax rates based on the different data sources for a consistent population of large corporate income taxpayers, as we do in the following section.

Various Measures of Taxes and Income Have Been Used to Estimate Effective Tax Rates

The two essential components of a methodology for estimating an average effective tax rate are the measure of tax liabilities to be used as the numerator of the rate and the measure of income to be used as the denominator.

---

[13]George Plesko employed a labor-intensive approach to link tax return data from IRS with financial statement data from Compustat, using each firm's employer identification number. Consolidation differences between financial statements and tax returns, along with other discrepancies, forced the author to drop many cases before arriving at his final study population of 1,116 firms. (George A. Plesko, "An Evaluation of Alternative Measures of Corporate Tax Rates," *Journal of Accounting and Economics* (2003).)

Tax Liability: Broader Measures Include Taxes Payable in the Future and to Other Governments

A common measure of tax liability used in estimates based on financial statement data has been the current tax expense—either federal only or worldwide (which comprises federal, foreign, and U.S. state and local income taxes); however, some studies have used the total tax expense, and others have used cash taxes paid during the year.[14] Corporations that filed Schedules M-3 for tax year 2010 reported a total of $185 billion in current U.S. federal income tax expense and $225 billion in total federal income tax expense, compared to the total of $187 billion in actual tax paid after credits that they reported owing IRS for that year.[15] Our data from IRS do not include a measure of cash taxes paid.

Income: The Treatment of Losses Can Significantly Affect Effective Tax Rate Estimates

The typical measure of income for effective tax rate estimates based on financial statements has been some variant of pretax net book income. Figure 3 shows the value of this book income measure for corporations that filed Schedules M-3 for tax year 2010 and shows the separate values

---

[14]The total tax expense is the sum of current taxes and deferred taxes. Deferred taxes represent estimated taxes that will be paid (or refunded) in a future year as timing differences between book and tax reporting reverse themselves and carryforwards are recognized. For example when tax depreciation is more rapid than book depreciation a company in effect postpones part of its actual tax liability on this year's book income because in the current year its net income for tax purposes (after the depreciation deduction) will be lower than its income for book purposes. The postponed taxes will be paid in later years when book depreciation deductions become larger than those for tax purposes. The amount of postponed taxes associated with current year income is reported as a deferred tax expense. Taxes which are reported as deferred in one year are included in current tax expenses and cash taxes paid in future years (which is why some studies choose to exclude them from their effective tax rate measures). The cash taxes paid, as reported in statement of cash flows or notes to the financial statements, represents what companies actually pay to the IRS in the current year; however, they do not necessarily relate to the current year's income. For example, those amounts can include additional payments for earlier tax years resulting from IRS audit adjustments. The actual tax liability reported on a corporation's form 1120 is the amount of tax that it actually owes to IRS for income earned in that tax year. The actual tax liability can differ from the current tax expense for a number of reasons, including the fact that corporations include an amount for "uncertain tax positions" in their current tax expenses. These amounts are not paid to IRS in the current year; they simply indicate to shareholders how much additional tax may have to be paid to IRS, such as taxes due as the result of a future audit.

[15]We use the term actual tax paid to refer to what corporations report as their income tax liability after credits on line 7 of Schedule J of Form 1120. The relationship between book and actual taxes can change from year to year, depending on economic conditions. For example the aggregate current income tax expense for Schedule M-3 filers in tax year 2006 was $310 billion, compared to $278 billion in actual taxes paid after credits.

for profitable and unprofitable filers.[16] Profitable filers had aggregate pretax net book income of $1.4 trillion while unprofitable filers had losses totaling $315 billion, resulting in total net book income of $1.1 trillion for the full population.[17] As these numbers suggest, average effective tax rates can vary significantly depending on the population of corporations covered by the estimate. The inclusion of unprofitable firms, which pay little if any actual tax, can result in relatively high estimates because the losses of unprofitable corporations greatly reduce the denominator of the effective rate. Such estimates do not accurately represent the tax rate on the profitable corporations that actually pay the tax. Some prior studies have excluded unprofitable corporations; others have not.

---

[16]We use the term profitable to refer to those Schedule M-3 filers that had nonnegative amounts for net book income reported on that schedule. To compute pretax net book income we start with the net book income reported in financial statements and add back in the total tax expense.

[17]In the other two years for which we had data for profitable and unprofitable filers aggregate losses were considerably larger. In 2009 the $619 billion of losses for unprofitable filers offset more than half of the $1.2 trillion of income for profitable filers, resulting in aggregate net income of only $568 billion. In 2008 the losses of unprofitable filers actually exceeded the income of profitable ones, resulting in an aggregate net loss for the full population.

Figure 3: A Comparison of Income Reported in Financial Statements and on Tax Returns by Profitable and Unprofitable Schedule M-3 Filers for Tax Year 2010

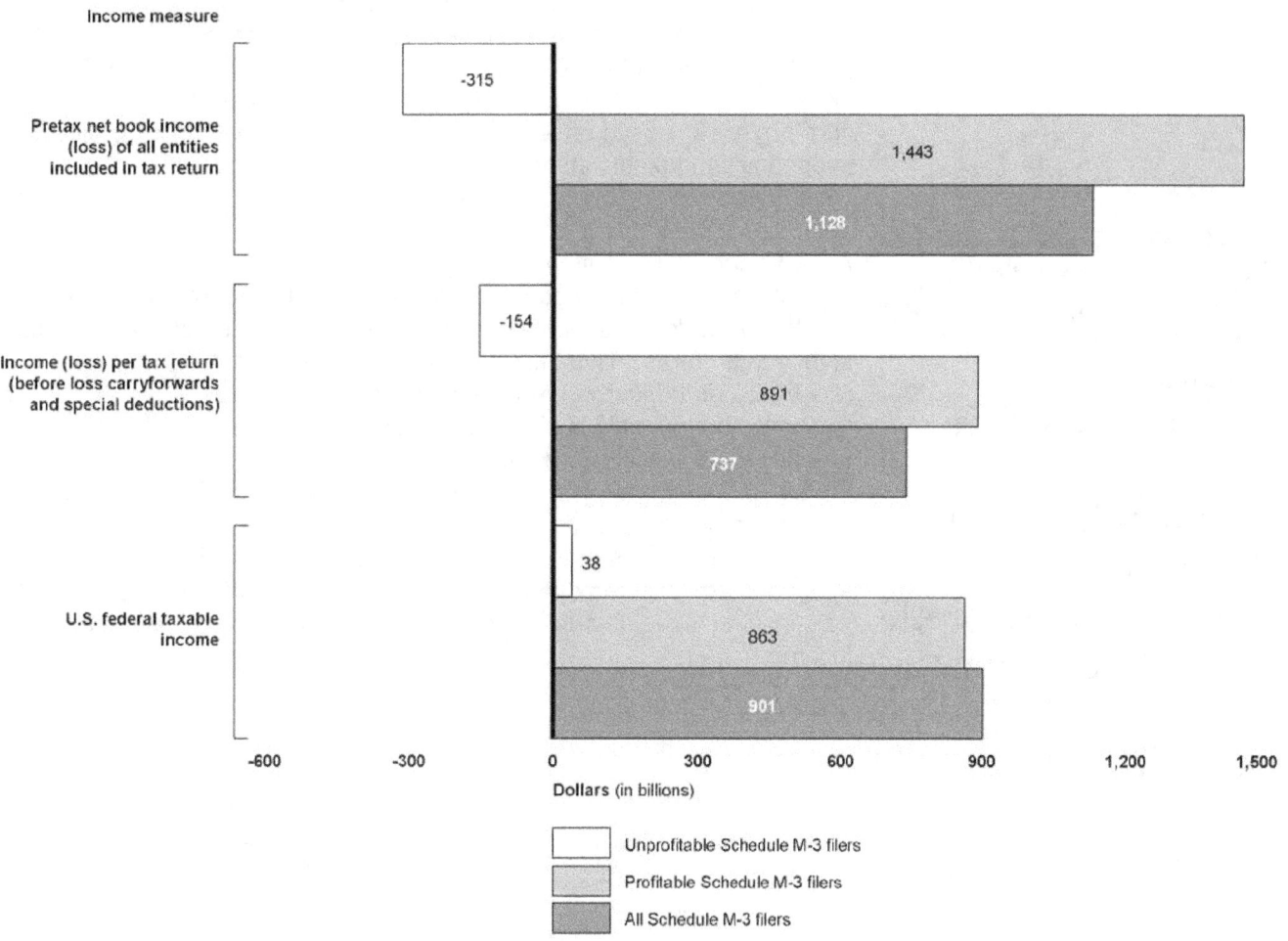

Source: GAO analysis of IRS data.

Figure 3 also shows the value of two income measures defined by tax rules for the same population of taxpayers. The first measure, income (loss) before net operating loss deductions and special deductions, is the tax return measure to which Schedule M-3 filers are required to reconcile their net book income (we refer to this measure as net tax income). It represents total income minus all deductions, except for losses carried over from other tax years and the special deductions relating to intercorporate dividends. The positive values of this measure for profitable filers, negative values for unprofitable filers, and net value for all filers are all of a lower magnitude relative to book net income.[18] The final measure shown in figure 3 is taxable income, which equals net tax income minus losses carried over from other years and special deductions. Taxable income is higher than tax net income for the full population of Schedule M-3 filers, even after the additional deductions, because it is defined to be no less than zero. Therefore there are no current-year losses to offset positive income amounts. For the profitable subpopulation taxable income is lower than net tax income.

The Average Effective Tax Rates for Profitable Large Corporations Were Well Below the Statutory Rate and Well Below the Effective Rates for All Large Corporations in Tax Years 2008 through 2010

For tax year 2010, profitable Schedule M-3 filers actually paid U.S. federal income taxes amounting to 12.6 percent of the worldwide income that they reported in their financial statements (for those entities included in their tax returns). This tax rate is slightly lower than the 13.1 percent rate based on the current federal tax expenses that they reported in those financial statements; it is significantly lower than the 21 percent effective rate based on actual taxes and taxable income, which itself is well below the top statutory rate of 35 percent.[19] The relatively low federal effective tax rate cannot be explained by income taxes paid to other countries. Even when foreign, state, and local corporate income taxes are included in the numerator, for tax year 2010, profitable Schedule M-3 filers actually paid income taxes amounting to 16.9 percent of their reported worldwide income.

---

[18]Some of this difference is due to the fact that some of the filers that were categorized as profitable on the basis of their book net income actually had negative tax net income, which offsets some of the positive tax net income for that subpopulation. The converse is true for the subpopulation of unprofitable filers. Also, net tax income reflects the deduction of state and local income taxes and foreign taxes that are deducted (rather than offset by credits); pretax book income is before these deductions.

[19]The book taxes and incomes that we obtained from the Schedule M-3 data represent the totals for entities included in the filers' tax returns. These amounts can be different from the totals reported in publicly available financial statements due to differing consolidation rules for book and tax purposes, which are discussed in the following section.

The Average Effective Tax Rates Based on Book Income Are Lower When Unprofitable Corporations Are Excluded

All of the effective tax rates based on book income for profitable filers are lower than the equivalent measures computed for all Schedule M-3 filers, shown on the right side of figure 4, because the inclusion of losses reduces the aggregate income for all Schedule M-3 filers. This difference was particularly large for tax year 2009 because the aggregate losses of unprofitable filers were considerably larger in that year than in 2010.[20] Aggregate book losses were even larger for tax year 2008; however, because these losses more than offset the income of profitable corporations, resulting in an overall net loss, we could not compute meaningful average effective tax rates based on book income for all corporations for that year.

---

[20]This fact explains how it is possible that during an economic downturn the number of corporations not paying taxes can increase at the same time that estimated average effective tax rates increase.

Figure 4: Average Federal Effective Tax Rates for Varying Populations of Schedule M-3 Filers and Definitions of the Effective Tax Rate, Tax Years 2008 through 2010

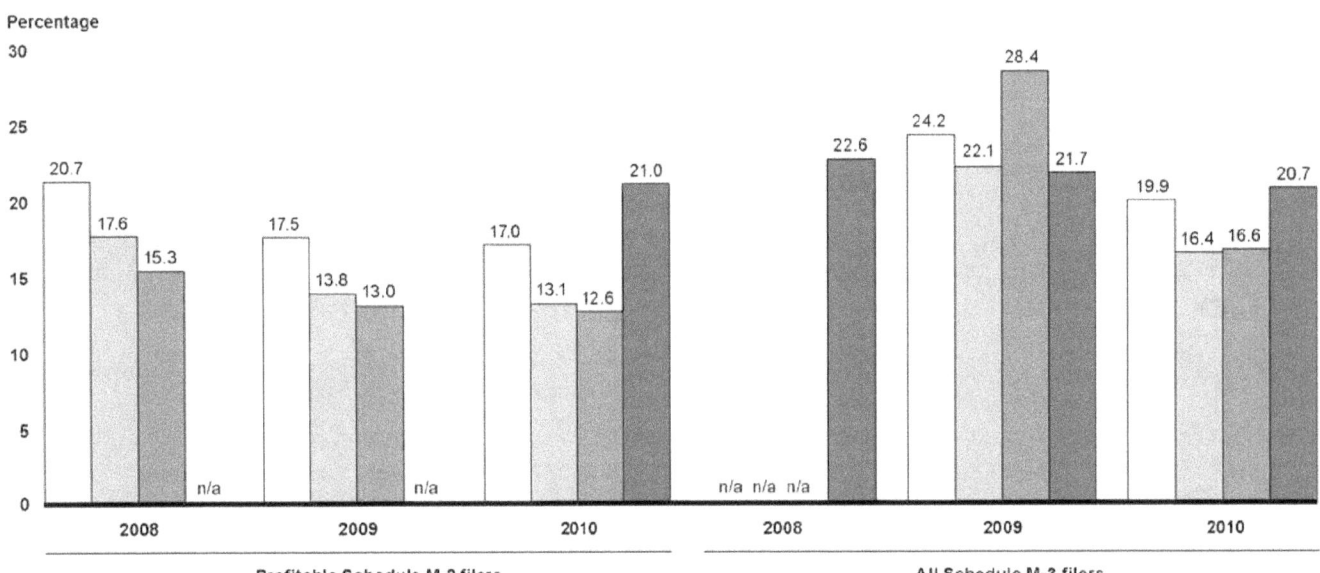

Profitable Schedule M-3 filers

All Schedule M-3 filers

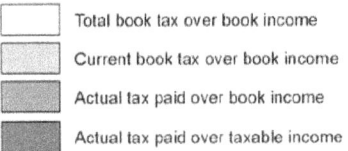

Definition of Effective Tax Rate

☐ Total book tax over book income

☐ Current book tax over book income

☐ Actual tax paid over book income

■ Actual tax paid over taxable income

Source: GAO analysis of IRS data.

Note: The measure of pretax net book income used in computing these rates is equal to worldwide net book income plus the total tax expense.

With access to only aggregated data, we were not able to provide any information on the distribution of effective rates across individual filers; however, past work we have done suggest that there could be significant variation in effective rates across taxpayers.[21] Nor could we compare effective tax rates for different types of corporations, such as U.S. controlled corporations and foreign controlled corporations.

The Average Effective Tax Rates for Profitable Corporations Were Well Below the Federal Statutory Rate Even When Foreign and State and Local Income Taxes Were Included

Past empirical studies comparing average effective tax rates across countries have focused on worldwide taxes (which add foreign and state and local income taxes to federal income taxes in the numerator). Our estimates for these worldwide rates ranged between 2 to 6 percent higher than the U.S. federal rates we present above, but the relationships between the different measures (total, current, and actual) within each year remained similar. (See fig. 5.) It is difficult to make close comparisons between our results and estimates from prior studies based on financial statement data because most of the latter estimates are averaged over multiple years for which we have no data. (See fig. 9 in app. I.) Our estimated rates for the full population of filers for tax year 2010 are generally lower than the estimates presented in earlier studies while our estimated rates for other years are generally higher.[22]

---

[21]In an earlier study, we found considerable variation in the U.S. effective tax rate on the domestic income of large corporations for tax year 2004. At one extreme, 32.9 percent of the taxpayers had effective rates of 10 percent or less, and at the other extreme, 25.6 percent of taxpayers had effective rates over 50 percent (GAO, *U.S. Multinational Corporations: Effective Tax Rates Are Correlated With Where Income Is Reported*, GAO-08-950 (Washington, D.C.: Aug. 12, 2008)). Moreover, in another study, we found that for tax year 2005 about 19 percent of the foreign-controlled domestic corporations that did not pay federal income tax and about 27 percent of the U.S.-controlled domestic corporations that paid no tax had positive net tax income (before loss carryforwards and special deduction). These corporations had ETRs of zero, which could have significantly reduced the average ETR for the population of profitable corporations. (GAO, *Tax Administration: Comparison of the Reported Tax Liabilities of Foreign- and U.S.-Controlled Corporations, 1998-2005*, GAO-08-957 (Washington, D.C.: July 24, 2008).

[22]Five out of the ten effective tax rate estimates shown in fig. 9 were computed for populations that excluded all corporations with negative book income.

Figure 5: Average Worldwide Effective Tax Rates for Varying Populations of Schedule M-3 Filers and Definitions of the Effective Tax Rate, Tax Years 2006 through 2010

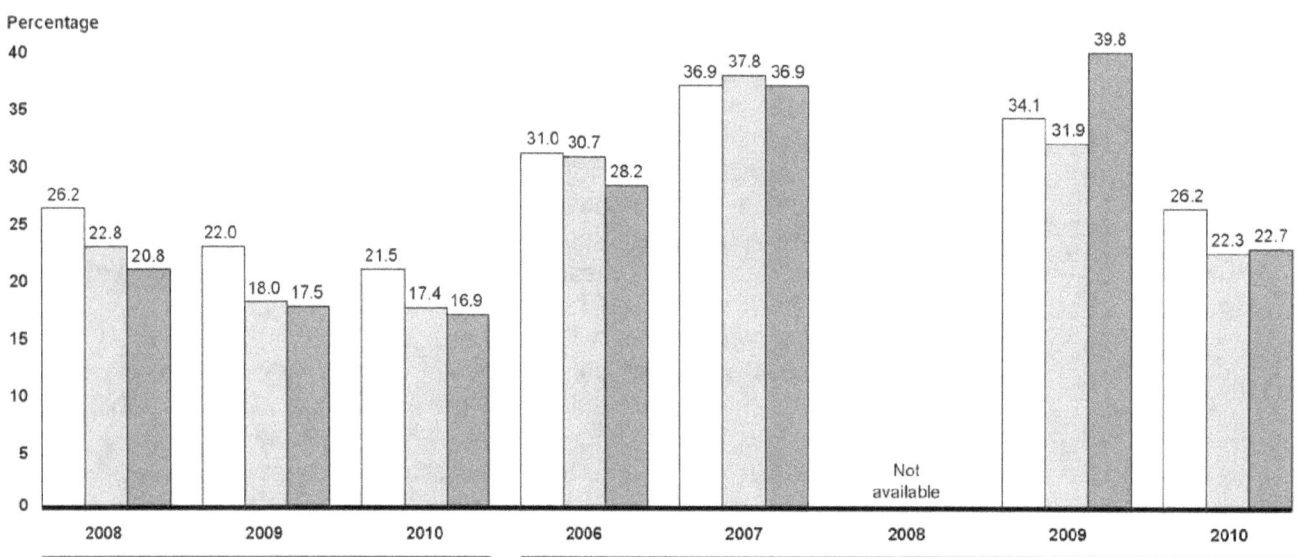

Source: GAO analysis of IRS data.

Note: The denominator for all of the effective tax rates in this figure is pretax worldwide net book income. The measure "Primarily actual taxes paid" equals the sum of actual U.S. federal and state and local income taxes paid, as reported on federal tax returns, plus the current foreign tax expenses and foreign withholding tax expenses from financial statements. We use the book amounts for foreign taxes paid, rather than the tax return amounts, because the latter does not include all of the foreign taxes paid on foreign income.

Financial and Tax Reporting Differ in Terms of Entities Included, Fundamental Treatment of Other Items, and Periods in which Certain Income and Expense Items Are Recorded

As noted above, it can be difficult to compare financial statements with tax returns because entities included under each type of reporting can differ.[23] IRS developed Schedule M-3 Part I to help delineate book-tax differences related to consolidation and to standardize the definition of the financial, or book, income of the tax consolidated group. As shown in figure 6, for tax year 2010 Schedule M-3 filers reported that they earned a total of $1.3 trillion from U.S. and foreign entities that were included in their consolidated financial statement but not in their consolidated tax returns (which, therefore, had to be subtracted out on the Schedule M-3). They also reported $420 billion in losses from such entities. (These losses also had to be subtracted out, meaning that net income increased by $420 billion.) In contrast, they reported less than $10 billion in either income or losses from entities that are included in their tax returns but not in their financial statements. These corporations also reported $762 billion in positive adjustments and $20 billion in negative adjustments relating to transactions between excluded and included entities.[24] The corporations must also report several other types of adjustments, such as for any difference between the time period covered by their financial statements and the period covered by their tax years, that they make in order to arrive at a final amount that represents the net book income or loss of all of their entities that are included in their tax returns. For tax year 2010, this population of Schedule M-3 filers reported a total of $1.1 trillion in net book income for entities included in their tax returns and a total of $300 billion in losses for such entities.[25]

---

[23]The thresholds for consolidating entities are different for book and tax purposes, so the entities included under each can differ.

[24]For example, adjustments are made to reverse the elimination of intercompany dividends involving entities removed at an earlier point on the schedule.

[25]The difference between this final income measure and the first income measure shown in fig. 3 is that this measure is after subtracting the total book tax expense, while the fig. 3 measure is before that subtraction.

Figure 6: Adjustments Reported on Schedule M-3, Part I to Determine Net Book Income of All Entities Included in Tax Return, Tax Year 2010

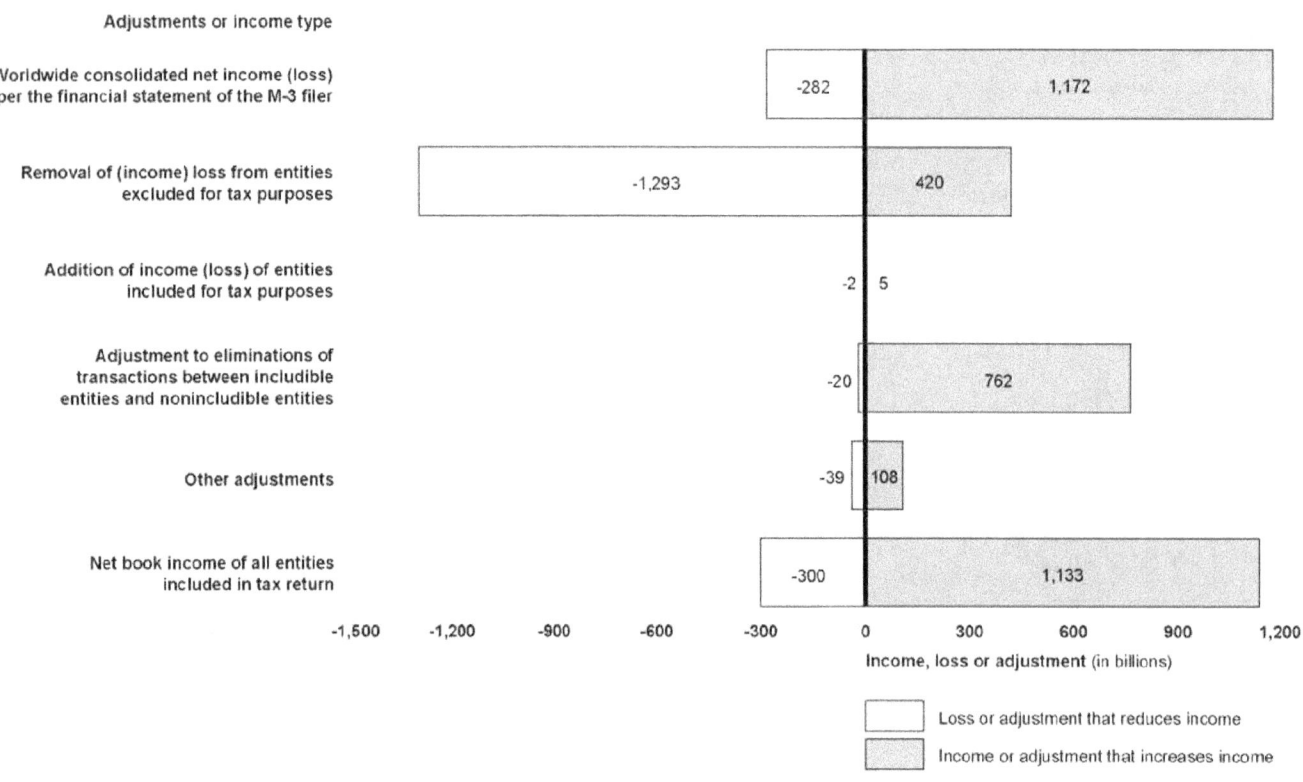

Source: GAO analysis of IRS data.

Schedule M-3 Parts II and III report book-tax differences related to income and expenses, respectively, for the tax consolidated group only. The largest category of differences for both income and expense items was "other." IRS officials told us that their reviews of the detailed documentation that filers are required to submit along with their Schedules M-3 indicate three broad subtypes of reporting in these other categories:

1. Some common income and expense categories have no line of their own on the M-3, so they have to be reported as other. This was the case for research and development expenses prior to 2010; those expenses now have their own line.

2. Taxpayers report miscellaneous items in these categories but do not provide details on what they include.

GAO-13-520 Corporate Income Tax

3. Taxpayers record items in these categories that clearly should have been reported on more specific lines of the M-3. The officials suggested some taxpayers do this because they do not take the time or trouble to fill out the form properly; others may be trying to hide details from the IRS.

As a consequence, there is over-reporting in the two "other" categories and under-reporting in some of the more specific categories. Figures 7 and 8 identify the 10 largest categories of book-tax differences for both income and expense items in tax year 2010.[26]

Book-tax differences caused by the inclusion of an income or expense item by one accounting system but not the other are known as permanent differences. One of the largest permanent book-tax income differences reported in tax year 2010 arose from the section 78 gross-up, as shown in figure 7. Section 78 of the IRC requires U.S. corporations electing to claim the foreign tax credit to gross-up (i.e., increase) their dividend income by the amount of creditable foreign income taxes associated with the dividends they received.[27] Given that corporations are not required to make this type of adjustment for book income purposes, the amount of any gross-up is a permanent positive difference between tax income and book income.

---

[26]These categories are ranked in terms of the absolute value of the differences for all Schedule M-3 filers. Tables 1 and 2 in app. III show the separate dollar amounts for the negative and positive, temporary and permanent differences in each category, as well as the net difference, which offsets the negative differences against the positive differences.

[27]26 U.S.C. § 78. Section 902 of the IRC permits a U.S. corporation that owns at least 10 percent of the voting stock of a foreign corporation to take an indirect credit for foreign income taxes associated with dividends that it receives from that foreign corporation. 26 U.S.C. § 902.

GAO-13-520 Corporate Income Tax

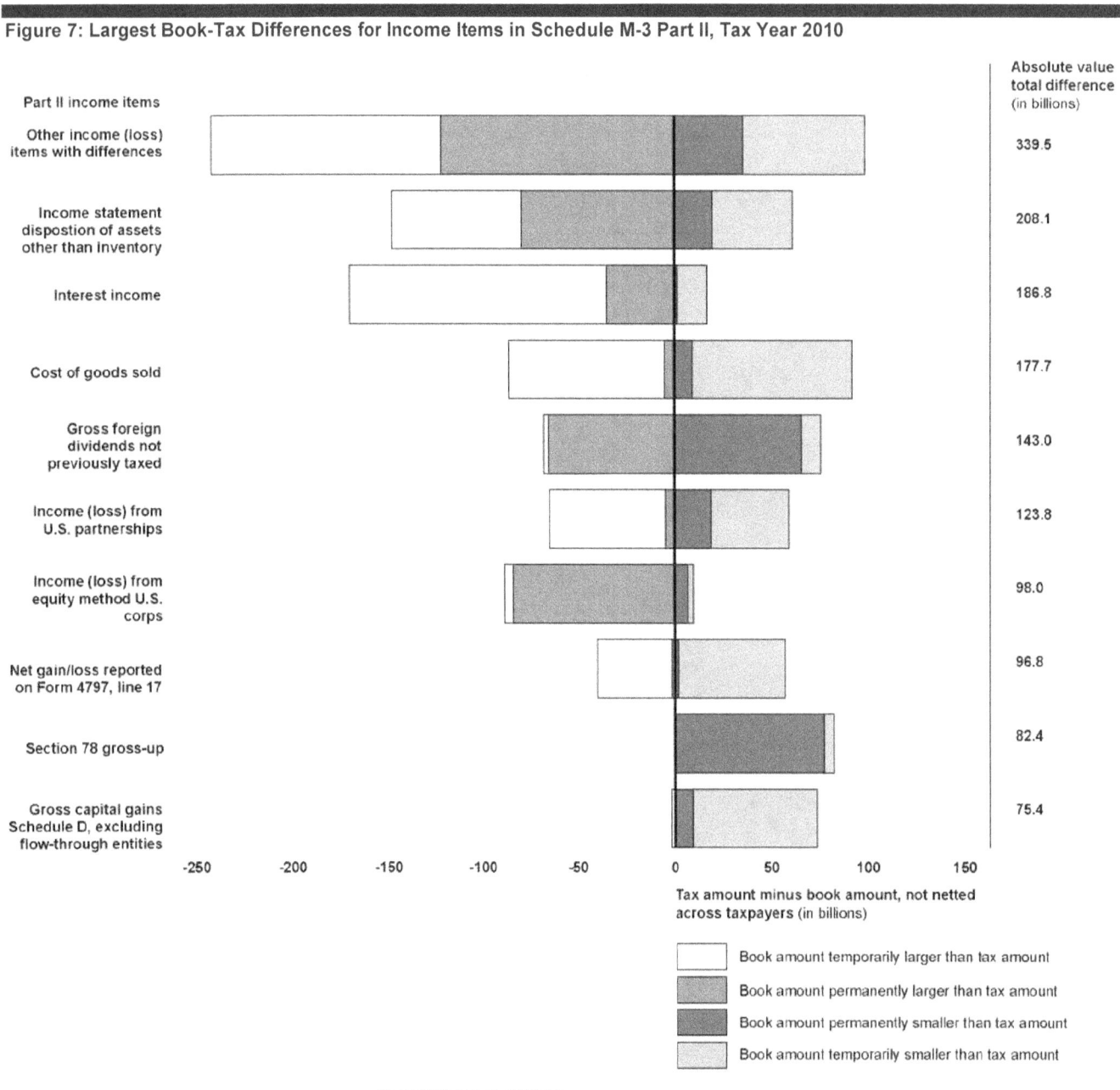

Figure 7: Largest Book-Tax Differences for Income Items in Schedule M-3 Part II, Tax Year 2010

Part II income items	Absolute value total difference (in billions)
Other income (loss) items with differences	339.5
Income statement dispostion of assets other than inventory	208.1
Interest income	186.8
Cost of goods sold	177.7
Gross foreign dividends not previously taxed	143.0
Income (loss) from U.S. partnerships	123.8
Income (loss) from equity method U.S. corps	98.0
Net gain/loss reported on Form 4797, line 17	96.8
Section 78 gross-up	82.4
Gross capital gains Schedule D, excluding flow-through entities	75.4

Tax amount minus book amount, not netted across taxpayers (in billions)

- Book amount temporarily larger than tax amount
- Book amount permanently larger than tax amount
- Book amount permanently smaller than tax amount
- Book amount temporarily smaller than tax amount

Source: GAO analysis of IRS data

Note: Within some of these categories a single filer can have both negative and positive amounts (e.g., positive income from some of its partnerships and losses from other partnerships). The aggregate positive differences shown for each category in this figure represent the sum of the net positive differences across those M-3 filers with net positive amounts in the particular category. Similarly, the negative differences represent the sums across all filers with net negative differences.

Book-tax differences caused by differences in the timing of when an income or expense item is recognized under each accounting approach are known as temporary differences because, over time, the total income and expense recognized for these items, as measured in undiscounted nominal dollars, is the same under the two systems. As shown in figure 8, a prominent temporary difference is depreciation. Accelerated depreciation generally result in depreciation deductions being reflected in taxable income earlier than when the depreciation expense for the same asset is recognized in net book income. Another significant temporary difference relates to losses from uncollectible receivables (e.g., bad debts). For book purposes, firms recognize losses on uncollectible receivables when the losses are probable and reasonably estimable. This may be applied in relation to individual receivables or groups of similar types of receivables, even though the particular receivables that are uncollectible may not be identifiable. In contrast, for tax purposes, firms must wait until a specific receivable is known to be uncollectible before it can be deducted.

Figure 8: Largest Book-Tax Differences for Expense Items in Schedule M-3 Part III, Tax Year 2010

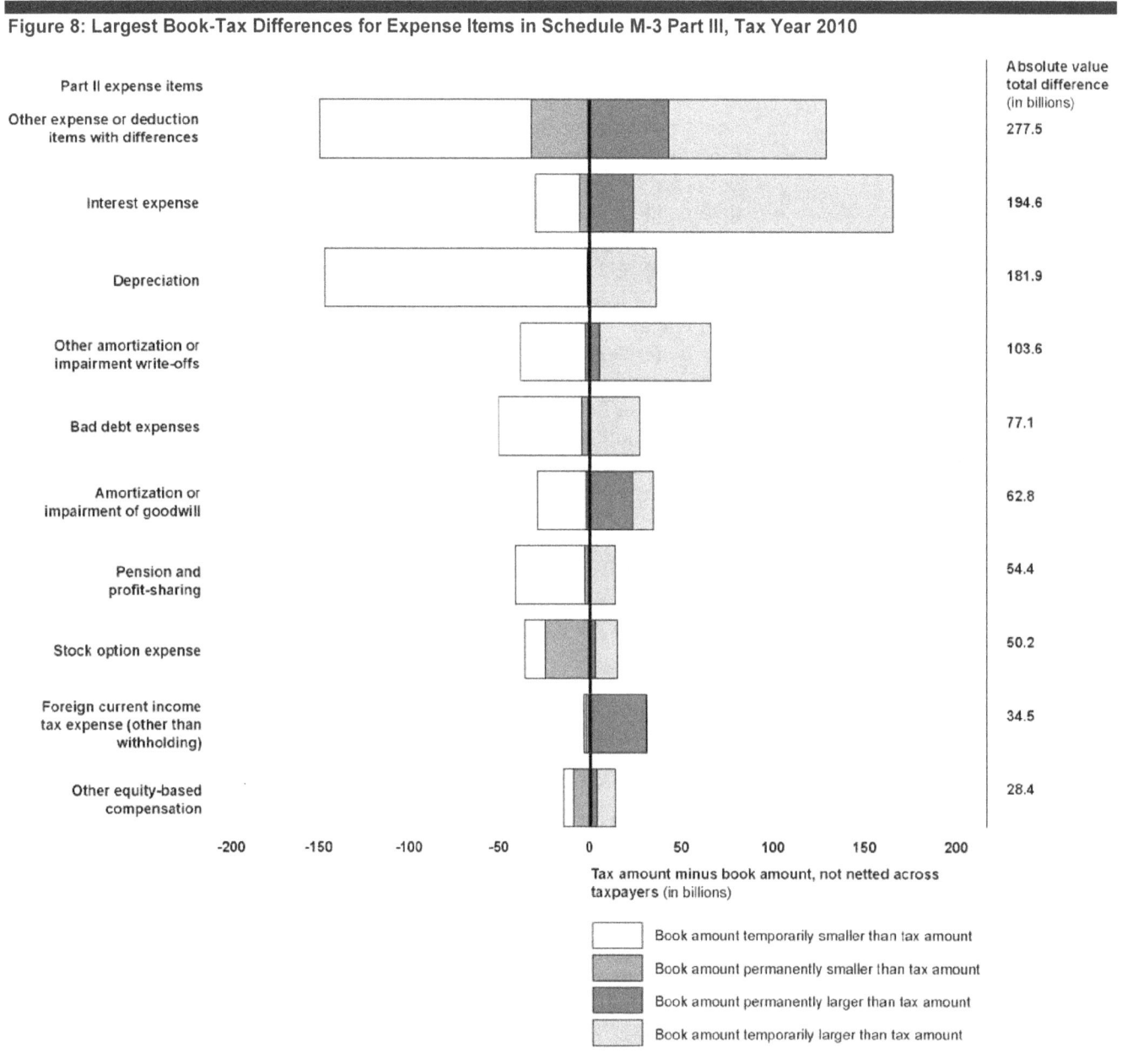

Source: GAO analysis of IRS data.

Note: Within some of these categories a single filer can have both negative and positive amounts (e.g., tax depreciation can exceed book depreciation for some assets while the converse can be true for other assets). The aggregate positive differences shown for each category in this figure represent the sum of the net positive differences across those M-3 filers with net positive amounts in the particular category. Similarly, the negative differences represent the sums across all filers with net negative differences.

The magnitudes of some book-tax differences varied significantly between 2006 and 2010.For example, the excess of tax depreciation over book depreciation increased from about $69 billion in 2006 to over $145 billion in 2010. As another example, the excess of tax income over book income relating to the section 78 gross-up increased from about $36 billion in 2006 to over $77 billion in 2010.

As the details presented in figures 7 and 8 indicate, the direction of the book-tax differences in all of the income and expense categories varies across corporations. The book amount is greater for some corporations, while the tax amount is greater for others. As a consequence, the aggregate net difference in many categories (shown in tables 1 and 2 in app. III) are significantly smaller than the absolute value of the differences. Moreover, the net difference is positive for some categories and negative for others. The offsetting of negative and positive differences across categories and across corporations within categories means that the relatively small difference between aggregate net book income ($833 billion) and aggregate net tax income ($737 billion) for the population of Schedule M-3 filers for tax year 2010 may hide considerable differences between book and tax income and between effective tax rates based on book income and those based on tax income for individual corporations. Given the aggregate nature of our data, we were not able to examine the range of potential differences across corporations.

Agency Comments

We provided a draft of this report to IRS on April 25, 2013, for review and comment. After reviewing the draft report, IRS provided technical comments which we incorporated as appropriate.

As agreed with your offices, unless you publicly announce the contents of this report earlier, we plan no further distribution until 30 days from the report date. At that time, we will send copies to interested congressional committees, the Secretary of the Treasury, the Commissioner of Internal Revenue, and other interested parties. In addition, the report also will be available at no charge on the GAO website at http://www.gao.gov.

If you or your staff have any questions about this report, please contact me at (202) 512-9110 or whitej@gao.gov. Contact points for our Offices of Congressional Relations and Public Affairs may be found on the last page of this report. GAO staff who made major contributions to this report are listed in appendix V.

James R. White
Director, Tax Issues
Strategic Issues

Appendix I: Summary of Selected Past Estimates of Average Effective Tax Rates Based on Financial Statement Data

Results from past studies, presented in Figure 9, use financial statement data to estimate average effective tax rates for U.S. corporations, employed pretax worldwide book income as the denominator of their effective rate, and covered at least one tax year since 2001.[1] As indicated in the figure, these studies used a variety of measures of worldwide taxes for their numerator. Five of the estimates were based on data that excluded all corporations with negative book income.[2] Most of the studies reported their results as averages across multiple years.

Other recent studies used aggregate measures of tax receipts received by the U.S. Treasury and profits before taxes from the Bureau of Economic Analysis's (BEA) National Income and Product Account (NIPA) data to estimate average corporate effective tax rates.[3] The BEA profits measure is created using an aggregate income amount using tax data adjusted by two components: inventory valuation adjustment and capital consumption adjustment. Due to the aggregate nature of the profits before taxes, the denominator includes corporations with positive and negative profits before taxes. Another recent study by Citizens for Tax Justice and the Institute on Taxation and Economic Policy used financial statement data but focused on the effective rate of the federal income tax on U.S. domestic income, rather than worldwide taxes on worldwide income. They estimated a three-year (2008 to 2010) average effective tax rate of 18.5 percent for a sample of 280 of the largest U.S. corporations.[4]

---

[1] These are all the studies we found as of March 2013 that met these criteria.

[2] The five are: PricewaterhouseCoopers, the two Markle and Shackelfords, Lee and Swenson, and the second Dyreng, Hanlon, and Maydew. Costa and Gravelle, who made use of Schedule M-3 data, excluded corporations if both their book net income and their tax net income were negative. The Hanlon and Maydew estimate and the first of the Dyreng, Hanlon, and Maydew estimates include corporations for which the sum of their net income over a 10-year period was positive.

[3] See, for example, Steven Maguire, *Average Effective Corporate Tax Rates: 1959 to 2005,* Congressional Research Service (Sept. 6, 2006); Martin A. Sullivan, "The Effective Corporate Tax Rate is Falling," *Tax Notes* (Jan. 22, 2007): 280-282; and Mark P. Keightley, *Reasons for the Decline in Corporate Tax Revenues,* Congressional Research Service (Dec. 8, 2011).

[4] Robert S. MacIntyre, Matthew Gardner, Rebecca J. Wi kins, and Richard Phillips, *Corporate Taxpayers & Corporate Tax Dodgers 2008-10* (Washington, D.C.: Citizens for Tax Justice and the Institute on Taxation and Economic Policy, November 2011).

Figure 9: Average Effective Tax Rates for Selected Studies on U.S. Companies, Using Worldwide Pretax Net Book Income

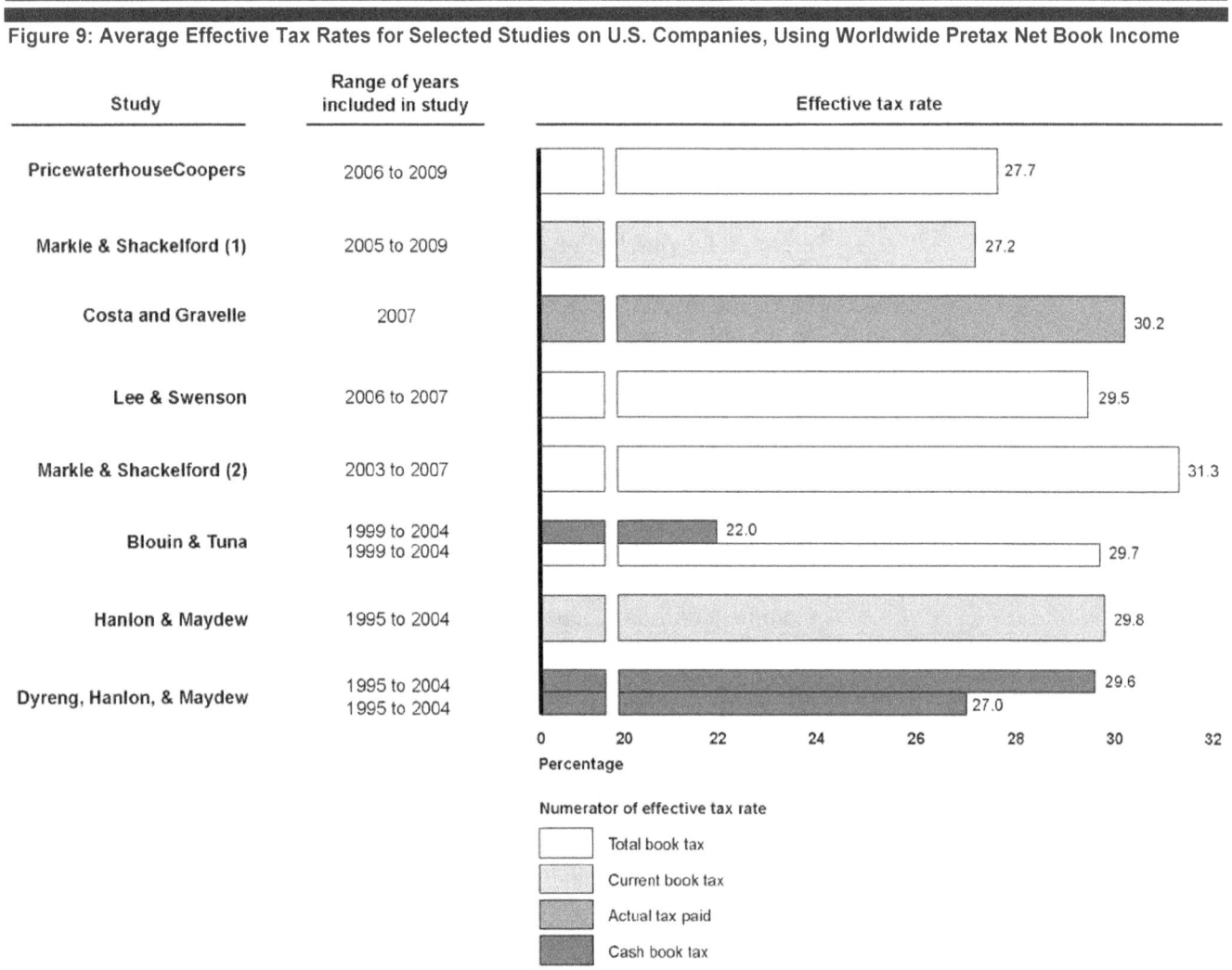

Source: GAO analysis of selected studies.

Notes: The full citations for the included studies are PricewaterhouseCoopers LLP, Global Effective Tax Rates (April 14, 2011); Kevin S. Markle and Douglas A. Shackelford (1), "Cross-Country Comparisons of Corporate Income Taxes," National Tax Journal, vol. 65, no. 3 (2012) 493-528; Melissa Costa and Jennifer Gravelle, "Taxing Multinational Corporations: Average Tax Rates," Symposium on International Taxation and Competitiveness, 65 Tax L. Rev. 391 (2012); Namryoung Lee and Charles Swenson, "Is It a Level Playing Field? An Analysis of Effective Tax Rates," Tax Notes International (May 25, 2009) 685-693; Kevin S. Markle and Douglas Shackelford (2), Do Multinationals or Domestic Firms Face Higher Effective Tax Rates?, National Bureau of Economic Research, Working Paper 15091 (June 2009); Jennifer L. Blouin and Irem Tuna, Tax Contingencies: Cushioning the Blow to Earnings?, Working Paper (April 2007); Michelle Hanlon and Edward L. Maydew, "Book-Tax Conformity: Implications for Multinational Firms," National Tax Journal, vol. 62, no. 1 (March 2009) 127-153; Scott D. Dyreng, Michelle Hanlon, and Edward L. Maydew, "Long-Run Corporate Tax Avoidance," The Accounting Review, vol. 83, no. 1 (2008) 61-82.

The two studies by Markle and Shackelford report their estimates separately for domestic and multinational firms. For each study we use data on the pretax book income of each subpopulation of firms to report a weighted average effective rate for the entire population.

Appendix II: Copy of IRS Form 1120, Schedule M-3 (Tax Year 2010)

<table>
<tr><td>SCHEDULE M-3
(Form 1120)

Department of the Treasury
Internal Revenue Service</td><td>Net Income (Loss) Reconciliation for Corporations
With Total Assets of $10 Million or More
▶ Attach to Form 1120 or 1120-C.
▶ See separate instructions.</td><td>OMB No. 1545-0123

2010</td></tr>
</table>

Name of corporation (common parent, if consolidated return)   Employer identification number

Check applicable box(es):   (1) ☐ Non-consolidated return   (2) ☐ Consolidated return (Form 1120 only)

                  (3) ☐ Mixed 1120/L/PC group   (4) ☐ Dormant subsidiaries schedule attached

Part I   Financial Information and Net Income (Loss) Reconciliation (see instructions)

1a Did the corporation file SEC Form 10-K for its income statement period ending with or within this tax year?
    ☐ **Yes.** Skip lines 1b and 1c and complete lines 2a through 11 with respect to that SEC Form 10-K.
    ☐ **No.** Go to line 1b. See instructions if multiple non-tax-basis income statements are prepared.
 b Did the corporation prepare a certified audited non-tax-basis income statement for that period?
    ☐ **Yes.** Skip line 1c and complete lines 2a through 11 with respect to that income statement.
    ☐ **No.** Go to line 1c.
 c Did the corporation prepare a non-tax-basis income statement for that period?
    ☐ **Yes.** Complete lines 2a through 11 with respect to that income statement.
    ☐ **No.** Skip lines 2a through 3c and enter the corporation's net income (loss) per its books and records on line 4a.
2a Enter the income statement period: Beginning MM/DD/YYYY Ending MM/DD/YYYY
 b Has the corporation's income statement been restated for the income statement period on line 2a?
    ☐ **Yes.** (If "Yes," attach an explanation and the amount of each item restated.)
    ☐ **No.**
 c Has the corporation's income statement been restated for any of the five income statement periods preceding the period on line 2a?
    ☐ **Yes.** (If "Yes," attach an explanation and the amount of each item restated.)
    ☐ **No.**
3a Is any of the corporation's voting common stock publicly traded?
    ☐ **Yes.**
    ☐ **No.** If "No," go to line 4a.
 b Enter the symbol of the corporation's primary U.S. publicly traded voting common stock . . . .
 c Enter the nine-digit CUSIP number of the corporation's primary publicly traded voting common stock . . . .

4a Worldwide consolidated net income (loss) from income statement source identified in Part I, line 1 . .	**4a**	
b Indicate accounting standard used for line 4a (see instructions): (1) ☐ GAAP (2) ☐ IFRS (3) ☐ Statutory (4) ☐ Tax-basis (5) ☐ Other (specify) _____		
5a Net income from nonincludible foreign entities (attach schedule)	**5a**	( )
b Net loss from nonincludible foreign entities (attach schedule and enter as a positive amount)	**5b**	
6a Net income from nonincludible U.S. entities (attach schedule)	**6a**	( )
b Net loss from nonincludible U.S. entities (attach schedule and enter as a positive amount)	**6b**	
7a Net income (loss) of other includible foreign disregarded entities (attach schedule)	**7a**	
b Net income (loss) of other includible U.S. disregarded entities (attach schedule)	**7b**	
c Net income (loss) of other includible entities (attach schedule)	**7c**	
8 Adjustment to eliminations of transactions between includible entities and nonincludible entities (attach schedule)	**8**	
9 Adjustment to reconcile income statement period to tax year (attach schedule)	**9**	
10a Intercompany dividend adjustments to reconcile to line 11 (attach schedule)	**10a**	
b Other statutory accounting adjustments to reconcile to line 11 (attach schedule)	**10b**	
c Other adjustments to reconcile to amount on line 11 (attach schedule)	**10c**	
11 Net income (loss) per income statement of includible corporations. Combine lines 4 through 10 . .	**11**	

Note. Part I, line 11, must equal the amount on Part II, line 30, column (a), and Schedule M-2, line 2.

12 Enter the total amount (not just the corporation's share) of the assets and liabilities of all entities included or removed on the following lines.

	Total Assets	Total Liabilities
a Included on Part I, line 4 . . . . . . ▶		
b Removed on Part I, line 5 . . . . . . ▶		
c Removed on Part I, line 6 . . . . . . ▶		
d Included on Part I, line 7 . . . . . . ▶		

For Paperwork Reduction Act Notice, see the Instructions for Form 1120.   Cat. No. 37961C   Schedule M-3 (Form 1120) 2010

Source: IRS.

Schedule M-3 (Form 1120) 2010   Page **2**

Name of corporation (common parent, if consolidated return)   Employer identification number

Check applicable box(es): (1) ☐ Consolidated group   (2) ☐ Parent corp   (3) ☐ Consolidated eliminations   (4) ☐ Subsidiary corp   (5) ☐ Mixed 1120/L/PC group

Check if a sub-consolidated: (6) ☐ 1120 group   (7) ☐ 1120 eliminations

Name of subsidiary (if consolidated return)   Employer identification number

Part II   **Reconciliation of Net Income (Loss) per Income Statement of Includible Corporations With Taxable Income per Return** (see instructions)

Income (Loss) Items (Attach schedules for lines 1 through 11)	(a) Income (Loss) per Income Statement	(b) Temporary Difference	(c) Permanent Difference	(d) Income (Loss) per Tax Return
1 Income (loss) from equity method foreign corporations				
2 Gross foreign dividends not previously taxed				
3 Subpart F, QEF, and similar income inclusions				
4 Section 78 gross-up				
5 Gross foreign distributions previously taxed				
6 Income (loss) from equity method U.S. corporations				
7 U.S. dividends not eliminated in tax consolidation				
8 Minority interest for includible corporations				
9 Income (loss) from U.S. partnerships				
10 Income (loss) from foreign partnerships				
11 Income (loss) from other pass-through entities				
12 Items relating to reportable transactions (attach details)				
13 Interest income (attach Form 8916-A)				
14 Total accrual to cash adjustment				
15 Hedging transactions				
16 Mark-to-market income (loss)				
17 Cost of goods sold (attach Form 8916-A)	( )			( )
18 Sale versus lease (for sellers and/or lessors)				
19 Section 481(a) adjustments				
20 Unearned/deferred revenue				
21 Income recognition from long-term contracts				
22 Original issue discount and other imputed interest				
23a Income statement gain/loss on sale, exchange, abandonment, worthlessness, or other disposition of assets other than inventory and pass-through entities				
b Gross capital gains from Schedule D, excluding amounts from pass-through entities				
c Gross capital losses from Schedule D, excluding amounts from pass-through entities, abandonment losses, and worthless stock losses				
d Net gain/loss reported on Form 4797, line 17, excluding amounts from pass-through entities, abandonment losses, and worthless stock losses				
e Abandonment losses				
f Worthless stock losses (attach details)				
g Other gain/loss on disposition of assets other than inventory				
24 Capital loss limitation and carryforward used				
25 Other income (loss) items with differences (attach schedule)				
26 Total income (loss) items. Combine lines 1 through 25				
27 Total expense/deduction items (from Part III, line 38)				
28 Other items with no differences				
29a Mixed groups, see instructions. All others, combine lines 26 through 28				
b PC insurance subgroup reconciliation totals				
c Life insurance subgroup reconciliation totals				
30 Reconciliation totals. Combine lines 29a through 29c				

Note. Line 30, column (a), must equal the amount on Part I, line 11, and column (d) must equal Form 1120, page 1, line 28.

Schedule M-3 (Form 1120) 2010

Schedule M-3 (Form 1120) 2010   Page **3**

Name of corporation (common parent, if consolidated return)   Employer identification number

Check applicable box(es) (1) ☐ Consolidated group   (2) ☐ Parent corp   (3) ☐ Consolidated eliminations   (4) ☐ Subsidiary corp   (5) ☐ Mixed 1120/L/PC group
Check if a sub-consolidated: (6) ☐ 1120 group   (7) ☐ 1120 eliminations

Name of subsidiary (if consolidated return)   Employer identification number

Part III Reconciliation of Net Income (Loss) per Income Statement of Includible Corporations With Taxable
Income per Return—Expense/Deduction Items (see instructions)

Expense/Deduction Items	(a) Expense per Income Statement	(b) Temporary Difference	(c) Permanent Difference	(d) Deduction per Tax Return
1 U.S. current income tax expense				
2 U.S. deferred income tax expense				
3 State and local current income tax expense				
4 State and local deferred income tax expense				
5 Foreign current income tax expense (other than foreign withholding taxes)				
6 Foreign deferred income tax expense				
7 Foreign withholding taxes				
8 Interest expense (attach Form 8916-A)				
9 Stock option expense				
10 Other equity-based compensation				
11 Meals and entertainment				
12 Fines and penalties				
13 Judgments, damages, awards, and similar costs				
14 Parachute payments				
15 Compensation with section 162(m) limitation				
16 Pension and profit-sharing				
17 Other post-retirement benefits				
18 Deferred compensation				
19 Charitable contribution of cash and tangible property				
20 Charitable contribution of intangible property				
21 Charitable contribution limitation/carryforward				
22 Domestic production activities deduction				
23 Current year acquisition or reorganization investment banking fees				
24 Current year acquisition or reorganization legal and accounting fees				
25 Current year acquisition/reorganization other costs				
26 Amortization/impairment of goodwill				
27 Amortization of acquisition, reorganization, and start-up costs				
28 Other amortization or impairment write-offs				
29 Section 198 environmental remediation costs				
30 Depletion				
31 Depreciation				
32 Bad debt expense				
33 Corporate owned life insurance premiums				
34 Purchase versus lease (for purchasers and/or lessees)				
35 Research and development costs (attach schedule)				
36 Section 118 exclusion (attach schedule)				
37 Other expense/deduction items with differences (attach schedule)				
38 **Total expense/deduction items.** Combine lines 1 through 37. Enter here and on Part II, line 27, reporting positive amounts as negative and negative amounts as positive				

Schedule M-3 (Form 1120) 2010

Source: IRS.

Appendix III: Detailed Data on Book-Tax Differences for Tax Year 2010

Table 1: Data for Largest Book-Tax Differences for Part II Income Items

Dollars in billions

Part II income items	Book amount temporarily higher than tax amount	Book amount permanently higher than tax amount	Book amount permanently lower than tax amount	Book amount temporarily lower than tax amount	Absolute value total difference	Net difference
Other income (loss) items with differences	$-119.7	$-121.2	$35.4	$63.2	$339.5	$-142.3
Income statement disposition of assets other than inventory	-67.9	-79.0	19.7	41.5	208.1	-85.8
Interest income	-135.2	-34.8	1.6	15.2	186.8	-153.2
Cost of goods sold (revised)	-80.5	-5.1	9.3	82.7	177.7	6.3
Gross foreign dividends not previously taxed	-2.3	-65.0	65.6	10.1	143.0	8.4
Income (loss) from U.S. partnerships	-59.9	-4.6	18.9	40.4	123.8	-5.2
Income (loss) from equity method U.S. corps	-4.6	-83.5	7.0	2.9	98.0	-78.3
Net gain/loss reported on Form 4797, line 17	-38.2	-1.4	1.9	55.2	96.8	17.5
Section 78 gross-up	0.0	0.0	77.6	4.8	82.4	82.4
Gross capital gains Schedule D, excluding flow-through entities	-1.7	-0.1	9.6	64.0	75.4	71.8

Source: GAO analysis of RS data.

Table 2: Data for Largest Book-Tax Differences for Part III Expense Items

Part III expense items	Book amount temporarily lower than tax amount	Book amount permanently lower than tax amount	Book amount permanently higher than tax amount	Book amount temporarily higher than tax amount	Absolute value total difference	Net difference
Other expense/deduction items with differences	$-117.1	$-30.9	$43.6	$86.0	$277.5	$-18.4
Interest expense	-24.1	-4.4	24.6	141.5	194.6	137.6
Depreciation	-145.1	-0.2	0.6	36.0	181.9	-108.8
Other amortization or impairment write-offs	-35.7	-1.4	6.2	60.4	103.6	29.5
Bad debt expense	-45.6	-3.5	0.6	27.3	77.1	-21.2
Amortization/impairment of goodwill	-26.9	-0.9	24.0	11.0	62.8	7.2
Pension and profit-sharing	-38.2	-1.7	0.4	14.1	54.4	-25.5
Stock option expense	-10.9	-24.0	3.5	11.9	50.2	-19.5

Part III expense items	Book amount temporarily lower than tax amount	Book amount permanently lower than tax amount	Book amount permanently higher than tax amount	Book amount temporarily higher than tax amount	Absolute value total difference	Net difference
Foreign current income tax expense (other than withholding)	-1.4	-1.5	31.2	0.5	34.5	28.8
Other equity-based compensation	-5.4	-8.5	4.7	9.7	28.4	0.4

Source: GAO analysis of RS data.

Appendix IV: Descriptions of Income and Expense Items with the Largest Book-Tax Differences

Income items	Description
Income statement disposition of assets other than inventory and pass-through entities	Differences in this category and the one below relating to Form 4797 arise from differences in book and tax reporting of gains or losses arising from the sale or other disposition of business assets. One such difference arises when accumulated tax depreciation for an asset is higher than accumulated book depreciation, which would make the gain upon sale higher for tax purposes than book purposes.
Interest income	Certain qualified interest income, such as that from municipal bonds, is exempt for tax purposes but must be reported as income in financial statements. Also some items may be treated as interest income for tax purposes but as some other form of income for financial accounting purposes.
Cost of goods sold	Cost of goods sold comprises numerous items, some of which have their own lines on the M-3, like depreciation and stock options expense, and other which do not. Among the differences reported on this line are those relating to differences in inventory accounting.
Gross foreign dividends not previously taxed	This line includes any difference between the amount of foreign dividends that corporations report on their tax returns and the amounts they report in their financial statements, unless those dividends have already been taxed by the United States.
Income (loss) from U.S. partnerships	This line relates to differences between the book and tax treatment of any interest owned by the filer or a member of the U.S. consolidated tax group that is treated as an investment in a partnership for U.S. income tax purposes (other than an interest in a disregarded entity).
Income (loss) from equity method U.S. corporations	This line relates to differences between the treatment of income and losses from equity investments under financial statement rules and tax accounting rules .
Net gain/loss reported on Form 4797, line 17	See description relating to income statement disposition of assets.
Section 78 gross-up	Section 902 of the Internal Revenue Code (IRC) permits a U.S. corporation that owns at least 10 percent of the voting stock of a foreign corporation to take an indirect credit for foreign income taxes associated with dividends that it receives from that foreign corporation. Section 78 of the IRC requires U.S. corporations electing to claim the foreign tax credit to gross up (i.e., increase) their dividend income by the amount of creditable foreign income taxes associated with the dividends they received.
Gross capital gains Schedule D, excluding pass-through entities	This line covers differences in the book and tax reporting of capital gains, other than those arising from partnerships and other pass-through entities.
Expense items	
Interest expense	One reason for differences on this line is that certain amounts that are treated as tax deductions for tax purposes are treated as some other form of expense for financial accounting purposes, or vice versa.
Depreciation	For tax purposes a firm depreciates its assets using the modified accelerated cost recovery system method, which allows the write-off of an asset at a much faster rate than straight-line depreciation, the most commonly used method for financial accounting purposes.
Other amortization or impairment write-offs	This category covers differences in book and tax amortization rules for items other than those relating to goodwill or acquisition, reorganization and start-up costs.
Bad debt expenses	Under Generally Accepted Accounting Principles, firms are required to estimate the proportion of sales that will ultimately become uncollectible and expense this amount in the same period as the recognition of the sale in revenue. In contrast, for tax purposes firms must wait until a specific receivable is known to be uncollectible before it can be deducted.

Appendix IV: Descriptions of Income and
Expense Items with the Largest Book-Tax
Differences

Income items	Description
Amortization or impairment of goodwill	Prior to 2002, goodwill was amortized over a maximum of 40 years for book purposes; after 2001 financial accounting changed to the impairment method, whereby goodwill is only written down if it is judged by management and auditors to be impaired. For tax purposes, goodwill was not deduct ble prior to 1994; since 1994 goodwill must be amortized over 15 years. These differences between book and tax treatments can be either temporary or permanent.
Pension and profit-sharing	This line covers all expenses attributable to any pension plans, profit-sharing plans, or any other retirement plans.
Stock option expense	A stock option expense generally is recorded in a financial statement as the estimated fair value of the option over the period of time that the stock option vests. The exercise of the stock option does not affect the corporation's net book income. In contrast, the IRC recognizes two types of stock options—qualified and nonqualified stock options. Firms cannot take deductions for qualified stock options (unless the stock is held for less than 2 years), although recipients get special beneficial tax treatment. For nonqualified stock options, the firm granting the option can deduct the fair market value when the recipient has an unrestricted right to the property and the fair market value can be reasonably ascertained.
Foreign current income tax expense (other than withholding)	This line shows the difference between the amounts of foreign income taxes that corporations report as expenses in their financial statements and the amounts that they claim as deductions for tax purposes. U.S. corporations typically claim foreign tax credits, rather than deductions, for most of the foreign income taxes they pay. Consequently, the book tax expenses typically far exceed the tax deductions.
Other equity-based compensation	Examples of the types of compensation that taxpayers are required to report on this line are payments attributable to employee stock purchase plans, phantom stock options, phantom stock units, stock warrants, stock appreciation rights, and restricted stock, regardless of whether such payments are made to employees or non-employees, or as payment for property or compensation for services.

Source: GAO summary based on IRS documents and accounting literature.

Appendix V: GAO Contact and Staff Acknowledgments

GAO Contact	James R. White, (202) 512-9110 or whitej@gao.gov
Staff Acknowledgments	In addition to the contact named above, James Wozny (Assistant Director), Elizabeth Fan, Robert MacKay, Donna Miller, Karen O'Conor, Max Sawicky, and Andrew J. Stephens made key contributions to this report.

GAO's Mission	The Government Accountability Office, the audit, evaluation, and investigative arm of Congress, exists to support Congress in meeting its constitutional responsibilities and to help improve the performance and accountability of the federal government for the American people. GAO examines the use of public funds; evaluates federal programs and policies; and provides analyses, recommendations, and other assistance to help Congress make informed oversight, policy, and funding decisions. GAO's commitment to good government is reflected in its core values of accountability, integrity, and reliability.
Obtaining Copies of GAO Reports and Testimony	The fastest and easiest way to obtain copies of GAO documents at no cost is through GAO's website (http://www.gao.gov). Each weekday afternoon, GAO posts on its website newly released reports, testimony, and correspondence. To have GAO e-mail you a list of newly posted products, go to http://www.gao.gov and select "E-mail Updates."
Order by Phone	The price of each GAO publication reflects GAO's actual cost of production and distribution and depends on the number of pages in the publication and whether the publication is printed in color or black and white. Pricing and ordering information is posted on GAO's website, http://www.gao.gov/ordering.htm. Place orders by calling (202) 512-6000, toll free (866) 801-7077, or TDD (202) 512-2537. Orders may be paid for using American Express, Discover Card, MasterCard, Visa, check, or money order. Call for additional information.
Connect with GAO	Connect with GAO on Facebook, Flickr, Twitter, and YouTube. Subscribe to our RSS Feeds or E-mail Updates. Listen to our Podcasts. Visit GAO on the web at www.gao.gov.
To Report Fraud, Waste, and Abuse in Federal Programs	Contact: Website: http://www.gao.gov/fraudnet/fraudnet.htm E-mail: fraudnet@gao.gov Automated answering system: (800) 424-5454 or (202) 512-7470
Congressional Relations	Katherine Siggerud, Managing Director, siggerudk@gao.gov, (202) 512-4400, U.S. Government Accountability Office, 441 G Street NW, Room 7125, Washington, DC 20548
Public Affairs	Chuck Young, Managing Director, youngc1@gao.gov, (202) 512-4800 U.S. Government Accountability Office, 441 G Street NW, Room 7149 Washington, DC 20548

Please Print on Recycled Paper.